FEET FIRST

FEET FIRST

Riding the Elder Care
Rollercoaster with
My Father

Jamie Legon

Feet First
Riding the Elder Care Rollercoaster with My Father

iUniverse books may be ordered through booksellers or by contacting:

iUniverse
1663 Liberty Drive
Bloomington, IN 47403
www.iuniverse.com
1-800-Authors (1-800-288-4677)

ISBN: 978-1-4759-7212-2 (sc)
ISBN: 978-1-4759-7213-9 (e)

Library of Congress Control Number: 2013901963

Printed in the United States of America

iUniverse rev. date: 2/28/2013

To Julie and Michael
and
all the children of aging parents

Contents

Gettin' old ain't for sissies ...

—Bette Davis, actress

Preface

I always told my father that he had to live to be at least a hundred years old, but I didn't know that he would actually almost *do* it. His unexpectedly long life forced me into a situation about which I knew nothing, where the results of my efforts were sometimes impossible to discern until much, much further down the line. It's my hope that this story will not only provide a few comforting laughs, but perhaps will also call attention to a few of the many issues of elder care. And I hope that it will reassure those of you already caring for your parents that you're not alone.

Introduction

To paraphrase an old saying, my father was a legend in his own mind, someone for whom aging was something that happened to someone else. But when his larger-than-life personality was forced to come to grips with old age, I got caught in the wake of a careening ninety-year-old man who never planned for anything and who happened to, at one time, have been my "boss."

I often had to make decisions for my father on the run and under duress, sometimes in situations where the gray areas far outnumbered the black-and-white ones. Affordable elder care proved to be a Byzantine netherworld without signposts or clear guidelines, and to say I was unprepared for it is a *major* understatement.

My experience with my father during the last years of his life was profound, disturbing, and enlightening—all at the same time—and the lessons of loving, giving, and forgiving were usually too difficult for me to understand while they were actually happening. I went through every phase of this journey with him, and at different times felt guilt, fear, angst, and anger. I felt guilty when I just didn't want to hassle with him and his situation anymore, and although I feared his bellicose and confrontational personality, I still felt angst over what was happening to him when I wasn't around. And I have to admit that my anger and frustration over Ellie's lifelong insensitive behavior was a constant component of the whole situation.

Perspective came much later...

Chapter One

"Your mother's had a stroke. Come right away." It was a Sunday afternoon in March when Ellie, my then ninety-year-old father, called to tell me that my mother, Gladys, eighty-five, was in critical condition and in the intensive care ward at Desert Hospital in Palm Springs, California. My wife, Julie, our two and a half-year-old son, Michael, and I jumped into our car and raced the two hours to the hospital from our home in Los Angeles. While Julie parked the car, Michael and I hurried in, just in time to catch the last wave of my mother's hand to her grandson and me, her youngest child. My mother's eyes focused on us for a few seconds before she lapsed into unconsciousness and, within a few weeks, her death. I knew that she had waited for us and only wondered whether she was telling us hello on our way in or waving good-bye on her way out. But, unknown to me at the time, her death and its aftermath would rule my life for the next six years.

Even though my parents had been married for more than sixty-one years, my father's grief was *amazingly* short-lived. He was completely over it in a couple of days. When I said

I missed her, he'd respond with a detached "Well, she was *your* mother." When Julie commented on how well liked my mother was, he replied, "Well, she kissed *everybody*, didn't she?" It was definitely strange, but I felt that, since he'd never been alone before, his survival mechanism might be kicking in. Still, I had flashbacks of meeting them for lunch not long before and noticing that they were holding hands.

My father's ninetieth birthday, one year before my mother's stroke

At the time that my mother died, my own family was in the process of a major job change and relocation from LA to San Francisco. I felt bad about leaving my father alone, and wanting to take care of him in the short time I had left before leaving Southern California, my wife, son, and I moved in with him, sleeping on a huge air mattress in the middle of his living room. It was a very difficult time for us—job stress plus relocation stress was now compounded by the death of my mother. Julie and I were constantly on edge, arguing frequently, and our attempt to save money by sleeping on the floor of my father's small apartment suddenly seemed utterly ludicrous.

About a week after we arrived, Julie and I were woken up in the middle of the night to see my father, dressed only in his underwear, pacing back and forth between the kitchen and his bedroom. He repeatedly swore, "Fucking whore!" and "That no-good dirty son of a bitch!"

I didn't know what was going on, but then I suddenly realized that—oh my God—he was talking about *my mother*! He cursed her and every member of her family—past, present, and future. Julie and I were frozen in place. We finally turned to look at each other, but we were both too stunned to say, or do, anything.

Ellie had no idea we were awake because, in his mind, he was whispering. My father was severely hearing impaired for much of his life, and his whisper constituted anybody else's scream. He kept repeating, "Fucking whore," and, "Let them all drop *dead*!" for over an hour, until he finally went back to bed. I stared at the ceiling, glad that Michael was still asleep, and debated whether or not I should have confronted my father. But I wondered whether, in the end, it was any of my business.

When he continued his angry diatribe into the next day, I had no choice. I thought, *Maybe he's in shock and is angry about being left alone.* But I was in mourning, trying to process my mother's death, and I couldn't take his unending negativity. He was watching a baseball game in the den and mumbling endless profanities about my mother, her sister, and even my *grandmother* when I confronted him: "Think whatever you want to think, old man, but don't ever say it out loud again."

He began to mount a feeble protest but then stopped and paused for a long moment. Still staring at the television, he said, "All right … I don't know … maybe I was just a flop in bed!"

I was too shocked and embarrassed to say anything.

My mother was a great beauty with natural white-blonde hair and blue eyes and possessed of an affectionate nature, while my father, though not handsome, had money and style. They were huge fans of Hollywood movies and movie stars and lived as if they were a real Hollywood couple— expensive clothes, the

Portrait of my mother, about 1950

best restaurants, and a house in one of the toniest areas of Long Island. Once, when my brother and I were little boys, we were on vacation in Atlantic City, New Jersey, and gathering in the lobby of our hotel for a formal dinner.

A woman and her husband approached my mother and said, "We're so sorry to bother you, Miss Turner, but … may we have your autograph?"

They actually thought that my mother was glamorous Hollywood star Lana Turner! Before my totally surprised mother could answer, my father took her arm, led her away, and said to the couple, "Miss Turner doesn't *sign* autographs."

*The Legon family in 1956. I had just woken up
after falling asleep in the car.*

Ellie wasn't a tolerant or patient person. During the cultural revolution of the '60s, our house was a major battleground—my older brother, Gary, and rock and roll on one side and my parents very firmly planted on the other. One day in the late '50s, my then teenaged brother repeatedly played the '45 recording of Little Richard's "Tutti Frutti" for an entire afternoon. After a few unheeded warnings to stop, Ellie went into his room, picked up the record, and smashed it to pieces over the edge of the desk, saying, "Get that nigger music outta here!"

My father's volatile personality and corporal punishment methods inspired far more fear than love. Ellie was volcanic and hot-tempered and, at his middle-aged peak, was built like

a bull—about five foot eight and over two hundred and ten pounds. When he was mad, he'd hit us in the body with an open backhand, correctly thinking that if he hit us in the face, he'd probably kill us. He'd say, "You're lucky! My father would've murdered me."

Although he'd brag to other people about his sons and their accomplishments, he rarely expressed affection

My father in his early forties

directly to my brother or me. To him, the congratulations of today weren't nearly as important as his expectations of us for tomorrow.

Notifying friends and family of my mother's passing was a strange walk down memory lane. Even the smell of their crumbling address book was a sense memory of my mother's mothballs and cedar blocks. The pages contained the names and numbers for everything from veterinarians for pets long dead to family and friends from yesteryear. Some recalled fond memories of great characters and good times, while others reminded me of my parent's stories of insults, hurt feelings, and misunderstandings. It contained the names of long-forgotten people from my own past—old girlfriends where, in the prehistoric days before cell phones, I might be reached. I saw the names of so many people I'd forgotten about whom, at the time, I'd cared so much about.

At one point, I reached an old couple in Connecticut that had been my parents' friends for many years. When the lady asked me how my father was doing, I said that he was doing surprisingly well and was already intent on getting on with his own life. "Well, that doesn't surprise me," she said. "You know, I don't think they ever *really* loved each other. I'm sure you understand, given all the things that had happened between them."

I had no idea what she was talking about, and for one millisecond, my curiosity threatened to overwhelm me. But I didn't want to take the bait and replied, "I just called to let you know that my mother is gone. Take care and good luck."

I hung up and recalled my father's profane late-night rant. But the bottom line was that I was older now, and I knew how the game was played. I didn't feel the need to know the gory details because, for me, our family history had already been written a long time ago.

Ellie wasn't a very sensitive guy. My mother put up with a lot, and it wasn't hard for me to feel sympathy for her, someone who might have had to look for love and pleasure elsewhere. I grew up in a swank but small house on Long Island, and I was a reluctant witness to the fact that their lovemaking lasted for no more than a minute or two.

I once saw my father hit my mother. I was about three years old or so when I went to check what all the screaming was about. I saw his raised arm come down on her, but I was a little too young to fully comprehend what was going on.

The next day, I asked my mother how she got "those black and blue marks" on her arm, and she bitterly replied, "Your father ... who else?"

Even though I was very young, I could immediately tell that she was sorry that she had said it. She tried to cover up her slip, but it was too late.

Money was my father's currency of affection. He was Big Daddy the Family Banker, and he let it roll. He was, for sure, a big spender—top hotels, expensive restaurants, the whole nine yards. Though my mother never had to work, she also never learned how to drive and was wholly dependent on my father. From my perspective, Ellie wanted us to fear him, just as he had feared his own father, an old-school Russian who took no prisoners.

My father was born in Brooklyn, New York, in 1911, the son of horse thieves and hustlers who arrived here from Russia by way of South Africa. During a horse-and-buggy ride from Long Island back to Brooklyn in about 1918 or so, my father and grandfather stopped near a field of grazing horses. My grandfather took a long look, pointed to a horse, and said, "That horse is blind." My father, already experienced with horses, looked the horse over and said, "He's not blind, Pop. He looks fine." To prove his point, my grandfather approached the rancher who was standing nearby and asked, "Is that horse for sale?" He didn't want the horse; he just wanted to see what the rancher would say. "Oh, you wouldn't want that one," the rancher said. "He's blind in one eye." When they got back in the buggy, my grandfather looked at my incredulous father and said, "How do you think I knew which horses to steal?"

Ellie's Brooklyn home was, by today's tight urban standards, a small farm. Built in 1915 by my grandfather at a cost of about eight thousand dollars, a pretty penny in those days, it was a giant brick Victorian on a corner lot and set on almost half an acre. Ellie, the youngest of four brothers and one sister, grew up in a yard filled with ducks, chickens, geese, goats, and even the occasional cow or two. He was last in the pecking order of an Old World family, where you spoke only when spoken to and the punishment for stepping out of line was swift and severe.

My grandfather was a successful salesman who, like my father, made and spent a lot of money. All his children had cars, clothes, and cash when that was only for the very rich. When my father met my mother through mutual friends, he was twenty-nine and my mother was twenty-four. According to my father, it was my maternal grandmother who strongly encouraged them to get married. Though I saw some affection between my mother and father, I never got the sense that this was any kind of fairy-tale love. For whatever reasons, he harbored lifelong and oft-stated resentments of my mother and her family.

Always a good provider, Ellie sold things on the black market—I have no idea what—during WWII before becoming a successful lingerie salesman. He never liked his name, which was unusual for a man. In school, they called him Eli or Elias, which he hated, so he tried on names like people change their underwear. At various times while growing up, I'd see mail for Allan Legon, Eli Legomsky (our Russian family name), Elias Legon, Allan Legion, and a few others I can't remember. His given name was Elias, though in his Yiddish-speaking household it was always Elya (pronounced EL-YAH), and he spoke Brooklynese, Yiddish, and Profanity with *great* fluency.

My brother, Gary, got to California from his home in the south of France a couple of days after my mother had her stroke. When he arrived at the hospital, I jumped up from my mother's bedside to give him a big hug. But we actually hadn't spoken to each other in over ten years. A lifetime's worth of residual bitterness, anger, and resentment had, for both of us, built itself into an insurmountable barrier. Whether real or imagined, bad timing and long-simmering undercurrents had created a miasma of hurt feelings.

A decade before my mother had her stroke, we'd had a major blowout, during which I'd said, "Screw you," to him, and he'd said, "Screw you," to me. That was the bottom line, and our estrangement had continued right up until that moment.

My relationship with my brother was, is, and always will be complicated.

Gary had already been king of the castle for seven years by the time I was born, and I think I might have been an unwanted interloper. I was far too young to be the friend and ally that he needed in his quest for 1960s-style teen independence, so his solution was to try and make me into a good soldier. Unfortunately, I wasn't very good at being a soldier and was too young and immature to appreciate his major good points—an already sizable intellect and a mature taste in clothes, food, art, and music.

He was, and still is, willful and strong-minded, and when I was young, he absolutely scared the pants off me. By the time I was only four or five, he was already beginning his "war" with my parents. After my father broke "Tutti Frutti" in half, Gary gave me a look that asked, *Whose side are you on?* and said, "Just remember—*I* am cool; they are *not.*"

Even though ten years had gone by, we picked up right where we left off with the kind of shorthand only siblings know. In the sitcom of my mind, I see myself as the eight-year-old of yesteryear, while he's still the fifteen-year-old boy known around our house as The General—only, in my mind, dressed something like George C. Scott in *Patton.*

The past was at least temporarily forgotten as Gary, forever logical and dispassionate, tried to rally the sad-sack troops he found. "She might come out of it," he'd say, though we both knew that probably wouldn't be the case.

My parents never made plans for *anything.* They were so superstitious about their passing that they thought, if they ever made out a will, they'd just keel over and die on the spot. They never discussed with Gary and I how one of them might live as a surviving spouse, and quite honestly, neither of us ever thought that my father would survive my mother anyway. She was easy, pleasant, and much more relaxed, so why worry? He'd *never* outlive her ... right?

Only a few days after her stroke, the hospital called and told us that my mother had to be moved to a full-care facility.

I was surprised—why so quickly? I met with the doctor, and he let me have it with a sledgehammer; she *had* to go because her stroke was *massive*, and *they could do absolutely nothing further for her.* His words sounded like a death sentence to me. I felt like I was in a Fellini movie—everyone's mouths kept moving, but I couldn't hear any sounds coming out.

I had no family to help me with Ellie. Gary was leaving for France within the next few weeks, and he made it absolutely clear that there was no chance he was going to put any time or energy into our father. In truth, over the years, they'd almost never seen eye to eye on anything.

Once, when Gary was home from college, my parents hosted a Passover dinner. In attendance were my mother's sister, Evelyn, and her husband, Harry; my maternal grandmother, Betty; and her third husband (very risqué in those days), Jack. During a discussion over dinner about the popular culture of the day (a hot-button topic in 1964), eighty-year-old Jack said that the Beatles were "crap."

My brother replied, "You don't know what you're talking about."

My father stepped in and said, "Apologize to your grandfather!"

Gary replied, "He's *not* my grandfather."

Ellie jumped to his feet and bellowed, "Apologize, I say!"

As my brother stood up to walk away from the table, my father took a swing at him. Gary fended it off and started backpedaling with my father in full pursuit.

"Stop!" screamed my mother, chasing after them.

"Ellie, you'll kill him!" yelled my aunt Evelyn, who was running behind my mother.

Gary continued backpedaling through the house and fending off the blows.

During this insanity, while they were backpedaling, I stepped in and tried to stop them (I was about twelve), but my father pushed me down on the couch. "Get out of the way," he growled; he was busy going after bigger game.

When things settled down a short time later, my mother and I visited Gary in his room. As he sat there staring blankly at the wall he said, "I'm never coming back as long as *he's* here."

Many years later, not a whole lot had changed.

Right before he left for France, Gary and I went to visit my mother for what would be his last time. He bent down and whispered in her ear, "It's okay, Mom. You can go now. *I'm* here." He was telling her that she had nothing to worry about because The General was back and in charge.

And wouldn't you know it, a day later my mother died.

I had already begun looking through my parents' giant hall closet (which contained more sets of sheets and towels than a Bed Bath & Beyond) when I heard Gary calling my name. We had been in the process of going over my parents' bills and bank accounts, and when I entered the kitchen, he had all the statements spread out in front of him. Without looking up he asked, "Are you aware that our parents owe over $230,000 on their credit cards?"

I did a double take—*$230,000? How could that be?* My parents had never said or done anything that would have led me to believe that they were so deeply in debt. Gary proceeded to detail a "rob Peter to pay Paul" scheme of over thirty credit cards that used one card to pay for another, paying for everything from breakfast at IHOP to medical and dental expenses. The majority of the cards were in my mother's name because, as my father's sight worsened with age, she had assumed the task of writing the checks. Gary and I had both known that money was tight, but we thought that meant that they were down to the end of their savings, not borrowing to stay alive.

Though my father retired with little savings and no pension, they thought that the $175,000 they got in 1971 when they sold our house on Long Island was going to be more than enough to allow them to live their lives out in a comfortable style. My father was already being slowly "retired" by his company after more than thirty-five years; they were trying to force him out in favor of younger, cheaper blood. My parents had *never* expected to live this long, and thirty years later, they found themselves still alive but with their money long gone. Social Security wasn't enough to cover the bills, while at the same time the cost of living was going up dramatically. And in a possible sign of a ministroke (and precursor of her fatal stroke three years later), my mother had told me that she could no longer remember how to cook any of her recipes. Eating at home was now too difficult for them, but eating in restaurants was costing more and more all the time. Their health started to decline, while their medical and dental expenses rose. And even though they were, for the first time ever, trying to live inexpensively, everything snowballed out of control.

Soon after my mother's death came the letters and phone calls from the credit card companies asking either my father or "the heirs" to pay the debt. The heirs? I thought it was a joke—the heirs to my mother's sheets and towels collection? Ellie's name was on some of the cards, but Gary and I had no financial ties to my parents.

We received telephone calls from collectors who acted like they were from the FBI—"We know where you live," they'd threaten. The harassment finally stopped after Gary and I wrote the various credit card companies an angry letter, telling them, in part, "We are frankly *amazed* that a man like my father, who's had no income for over thirty-five years, and has no savings to speak of, would be given this amount of credit. You make risky loans to unqualified people and then harass others who aren't responsible to pay for them."

For them, it was just business as usual.

Several times during the decade preceding my mother's stroke, my parents had asked Gary and me for money. When we asked them why, they'd say, "If you have to ask us what we need it for, then just forget it." Or they'd say, "We're just short this month. If you don't want to give it, then don't give it!"

Guilt works every time, and since Gary and I had the money, we gave it to them and left it uneasily at that.

During the period when Gary and I weren't speaking, we only communicated by fax, and never had any conversations about our parents (which might have brought their circumstances to light). We even bought my mother and father a car without a word passing between us.

After my mother's stroke, Gary and I had to force my father to allow us to look at his finances and obligations. I had been completely wrong in my financial estimation of my parents—they were broke, and in their desperation to stay afloat, they had asked us for money. Undoubtedly, the shame of their financial failures had prevented them from letting us know what was really going on. When we confronted my father about it after my mother's death, he insisted that, not *only* was there nothing wrong with what he and my mother had done, he intended to continue writing the necessary checks to keep his small-time credit card Ponzi scheme going. When we tested him to see if he could actually *write* a check, he couldn't even see the signature line.

We explained to him that bankruptcy was the only way out of this mess, but he wouldn't consider it. He felt that he had worked hard all of his life and that all he was doing now was simply cashing in on his excellent credit rating. At this point still in control of his faculties, he simply saw nothing morally or legally wrong with any of it—"Now's when I need it," he'd snap. "What's wrong with that?"

Exhausted from the ordeal of my mother's stroke, Gary and I allowed him his charade for a little while longer. But soon thereafter, my father was indeed forced to declare bankruptcy. He had no assets and nothing but debt, but having to declare publicly that he couldn't keep his financial ship afloat rankled him no end. Walking into bankruptcy court, he said "I could get a half a million if I wanted to!"

Chapter Two

Ellie made it clear that he'd rather die in Palm Springs than live anywhere else. The hot, desert weather was like springtime in Paris for his ancient circulatory system—the hotter the better. He generally kept the temperature of his apartment somewhere north of 85 degrees, and we'd sit around and sweat while he exclaimed how comfortable it was. "It may be a little hot out there, but in here? It's bee-eau-ti-ful." He maintained that the only possibility of moving was if I provided him with a butler and a separate home on an estate. "Well, *that* I would consider," he said.

It was 116 degrees the day Julie, Michael and I left Ellie and moved to San Francisco. Though we had only been with him for five weeks, I could see his decline even during that short period. His eyesight seemed to worsen by the day, and his already very limited hearing was diminishing. My father was no fitness buff; the only physical thing he ever did in his life was hose the leaves off the driveway. I doubted whether his indomitable will power and stubbornness were going to be enough to keep him going, so I told him that I'd arrange for some kind of outside help.

"No way," he said, "I don't need any help. No stranger is coming into *my* apartment!" This was the stance of a guy who had never so much as cooked a meal for himself in his entire life. Despite the fact that he needed help more than ever, his I-don't-need-anybody attitude was going to keep people away in droves. My brother had already said many times, "The only way he's going to leave that apartment is feet first."

He seemingly did all right for a while. But when we accompanied him to his favorite restaurant during one of our early visits from Northern California, the staff quietly told me of repeated episodes of choking and Heimlich maneuvers. It wasn't the first time that this was an issue. Even before my mother died, my father had problems with swallowing (a not-uncommon consequence of advanced aging). Anything, even a scrambled egg (let alone his favorites like pastrami and corned beef), could cause him to choke. He was so starved for the hot meal that he couldn't make for himself that sometimes he choked simply because he wolfed his food down so quickly. But he didn't care and continued to order his difficult-to-eat favorites.

Meals on Wheels, you say? Forget it. "I won't eat that crap" was his perennial response.

When my brother and his wife would come in from France for their once-every-year-or-two, two-day visit to Palm Springs, we'd gather at the local deli with my father. Sometimes he was in a great mood, but when he wasn't, watch out. Everybody was a no-good son of a bitch, or he'd loudly demand, "Where the hell is the waiter?"

At that point, my brother would lean over to me and whisper, "Order him the pastrami."

Heartbreakingly, the only thing he wanted to know was "When are you coming here?"

Visiting him was impossible; I was shooting a show (a 24-7 job) for months on end and just couldn't get away. I called him daily (if I didn't, he had me paged while I was on the set, usually in the middle of a shot), but most of the time he could barely hear me. Sometimes I had to talk so loudly that the entire cast and crew heard me and thought I was insane. Once, our conversation got *so* loud that everyone thought I was abusing my, to quote some crew members, "poor, old father." I never told them that it was probably the other way around.

If he was well rested and well fed, the hearing in his "good" ear allowed him to have a semi-normal conversation (the hearing in his other ear had completely deteriorated years before). He'd had ear infections as a child (around 1915), and standard procedure at that time was to pour hot olive oil into the ear canal. My father often told me that his hearing was never the same after that.

If he was tired or under the weather, forget it; he couldn't hear me at all. Shouting into the phone just turned speech into noise and made Ellie think I was angry with him even when I wasn't (although sometimes I was). His hearing aids, the only things still connecting him to the real world, were frequently failing because of constant use at ever-higher volume settings. On top of it, his vision was continuing to deteriorate. No magnifying glass was strong enough to allow him to continue to do his beloved crossword puzzle, and the crucial regular exercising of his mind was quickly becoming a thing of the past.

The apartment complex where my parents lived was a low-slung Palm Springs modern, the units either facing each other or set side-by-side. There was *zero* privacy, and now that my father was alone, the well-meaning neighbors started to take an interest in "the son who comes to visit with his family." On one occasion, a large man whose stomach arrived well before the rest of him approached me in the parking lot. Introducing himself as Larry, he asked, "Are you aware that your father is continuing to drive?"

I thought, *Uh-oh*, and defensively said that "of course" I was.

He said, "Well, we felt you should know that my wife and I saw Ellie almost kill a kid. He can't see where he's going anymore, and he almost ran the kid over. You know, it's one thing if Ellie dies in a traffic accident—he's already lived almost ninety-two years—but what if he kills someone who's only nineteen?"

I knew Larry was right and decided to confront my father about his driving.

I always took my father's driving ability for granted. He had been an expert driver for over seventy-five years and had driven safely until well into his late eighties. But shortly before my mother died, she had mentioned to me that he couldn't "see the road as well as he used to."

As far as Ellie was concerned, his driving was just *fine*. I must admit that the very idea of taking my father's keys away was a total nightmare for me. I already knew that he didn't respect me very much; I had lived my bachelor lifestyle longer than most, had a child when I was in my late forties, was only modestly successful financially, and didn't even legally marry until my son was already four years old. My brother married young, had a stable marriage with no kids and a relatively profitable financial life, and was able to retire early. In my father's eyes, I was the forever-young bon vivant of yesteryear, the sporting bachelor living the Hollywood high life of endless possibilities.

The conversation about driving went on for days that turned into weeks. "What? What did you say? What the hell are you talking about? I don't need to stop driving. You're out of your mind!"

But, when he eventually recognized that the issue wasn't going away, he gave in with a resigned, "All right, already!"

The problem was that, no matter who I found to help him cook, clean, or drive, the situation always ended up like a *Seinfeld* episode. Any outside help, whether male or female, young or old, was either "stealing from me," or "one of the dumbest son of a bitches who ever lived." He found fault with everything and everybody. Nobody was good enough.

As his anger and frustration grew, I countered with patience and understanding. That effort amounted to a nice try but no cigar; he only wanted me to help him if I was willing to act as angry as he did. The following is an actual exchange between him and me about calling the hearing aid guy:

ELLIE. Jamie, call that goddamn son of a bitch and tell him I think he's a lying bastard!

ME. Pop, that's crazy. I can't do that.

ELLIE. Are you calling me crazy?

ME. Dad, I didn't say you're crazy. I said *it's* crazy.

ELLIE. Who the hell are you to call me crazy?!!!

ME. *I'm going to kill myself*!

Ellie was a bra and girdle salesman who should've been an actor. He loved Hollywood, and he always lived his life "in character." Even at his advanced age, he still liked to play a few favorite roles, among them the Big Spender and the Sharp Dresser.

Ellie swore up and down that he wasn't going to let anyone into his apartment. I told him, "Dad, you're over ninety years old. Stop insisting that you don't need anyone."

He roared back, "Who the hell do you think you are? You're not my boss! I'll do whatever the hell I want to do!" And there it was—in his eyes, I was still just his little boy, even though at that point in time I was almost fifty years old, with a twenty-five-year career and a three-year-old son.

No matter how many times I told him that I'd pay for his taxis, Ellie refused to call one. He said, "I don't care! It's too damn expensive!" I think the real reason was that he wanted to prove his ability to survive on his own terms.

The only other transportation option was the elderly bus service, from which I purchased a prepaid, use-any-time bus pass. But, too impatient to wait for the bus, Ellie preferred to finagle rides from customers leaving the coffee shop adjacent to the bus stop.

Without my mother around, he didn't eat properly or drink anything but diet soda. Bacteria were building condos on his bathroom and kitchen floors, and when asked why he let the sliced meats sit on the counter for days on end, he'd say, "They were too cold in the refrigerator! They had no *taste!*" To my father, bacteria referred to the back room of a cafeteria.

My mother had been the buffer zone between Ellie's demanding personality and the rest of the world, and now that she was gone, everything was coming unglued. Making his own appointments and getting to doctors was very difficult, doing his laundry was too demanding, and cleaning his apartment was nearly impossible. And then came the big, looping curveball—he began having hallucinations.

At first, I didn't understand what was going on. When we talked on the phone, he told me about people coming into his apartment and refusing to leave. He was fairly cantankerous, so I thought he had probably gotten into an argument with one of his neighbors. "No, no, nothing like that!" he insisted. "They just came into my bedroom and wouldn't leave!"

When I asked who "they" were, he began reciting the names of people already dead. I did my best to reassure him—and myself—that the hallucinations were only dreams and would soon stop. But the truth was that I wasn't ready to admit that the effects of advanced aging had now taken a major toll on my father.

Early on, when I explained to Ellie that his visions weren't real, he'd immediately snap back into reality. "Oh, how could I be so stupid!" he'd say. He understood that it was all in his mind and hoped that it would just go away. But that didn't last long, and it soon became increasingly difficult for him to differentiate between reality and fantasy.

Late one night, my father called and said, "I finally had to call the cops on these people!"

I said, "Cops? What's going on?"

He replied, "Well, I figured that, since they wouldn't get out, the hell with them. I'll just call the police!"

In the hope that he would come back to reality—I was still in major denial—I tried reasoning with him and asked how anyone could possibly get into his bedroom.

"They came in through the walls! How the hell else could they've gotten in?" he said.

He was absolutely serious, but up until that moment, he'd never been delusional enough to call anyone during an episode. He cried into the phone, "Jamie, when are you coming here?" as if I could protect him.

I felt like I was running a sprint in a swamp wearing cement boots. Every day brought more disturbed phone calls from him, but I had no idea what to do. His dementia came and went in waves, and was almost always worse at night. During the day he was often relatively normal, asking about our jobs and schedules or his grandson. He responded cogently to my questions, and engaged easily in conversation. But the fact that he lived alone with little or no social contact, now compounded by the encroaching dementia, made it a situation where he had no behavioral norms to adhere to. Without my mother there to calm him down, he acted out his anger and frustration at the drop of a hat. And despite reminding him that, more than ever, he needed the help of the people nearby, he said, "I couldn't care less. Let 'em all drop dead!"

Ellie never lost his salesman's ability to charm people when he wanted (or needed) to. He occasionally used his brassiere collection as a bartering tool, giving them to neighbors when he needed favors or handing them out to the hostesses at restaurants to get quicker service. When he asked them, as only he could after a lifetime of selling bras, what their bra size was, they were thoroughly tickled even while being totally embarrassed.

My father was a Republican without the money—a social conservative for whom the Golden Rule meant that he who has the gold rules. He never thought much of my relatively anonymous Hollywood career producing and directing television commercials and videos.

Taking advice from me was out of the question for him; I just wasn't *successful* enough.

Like Charlie Chan, Ellie only respected his number one, far richer, son. On several occasions, I asked Gary to call my father and try and make him understand that he needed medical help. But, right on cue, every time they spoke, my father suddenly became as sharp as a tack, always giving my brother the Disney version of what was actually going on. "Oh, I'm fine! It's nothing!" he'd assure Gary. My father was too embarrassed to ask for help or advice from his eldest son. He only wanted help from me because, frankly, he never really cared what I thought one way or the other.

Since he saw any outsider as an intruder, nobody I hired to help him with his apartment, to drive him around, or to run his errands lasted more than two weeks. Unmoved by my pleas to calm down, he quickly alienated everyone around him, from formerly sympathetic neighbors to the hearing aid guy. No help was good enough ("They're morons!"), so he ended up with little or no help at all.

I was going crazy, waking up in the middle of the night feeling really anxious. I tried Valium. I tried alcohol. I tried everything, but nothing worked. Though my wife was supportive, neither one of us had any answers. Providing meaningful care from a distance was impossible, and throughout all this, my brother would occasionally call me and say, "I'm telling you, *don't answer the phone!*"

Gary always gloried in his differences with my parents. During his first year of college, he went to my father and asked for five hundred dollars. That was a *lot* of money in those days, and my father asked Gary to join him in his private bathroom for a little chat. After they closed the door, I crept up to listen.

In understanding tones, my father asked my brother, "What happened? Did you knock up some girl?"

Gary replied, "Well, no; actually, it's for a drug deal gone bad, and the drug dealer said that he'd kill me if I didn't pay him the money." Anybody else would've taken the easy way out and said, "Yeah, Dad. That's it," knowing that an unwanted pregnancy was something my father could understand. Not Gary.

Ellie exploded in rage, screaming, "You little son of a bitch!"

I ran.

My father started having dexterity and functionality problems with his fingers, and making the necessary adjustments to his hearing aids was becoming more and more difficult. As his hearing got progressively worse and communication on the phone grew tougher, his patience all but disappeared. Old frustrations surfaced about past events, perceived slights, my mother, current friends, me, and even people who were already dead. Everyone was a "son of a bitch," and even Julie, normally a great believer in family standing by each other no matter what, began to resent the constant negativity and unrelenting wear and tear on me.

Even in the best-case scenario, I could only visit him every three to five weeks, and sometimes, our schedules didn't allow for any visits at all. The drive was horrible—a grueling, sixteen-hour round trip of endless highway, ugly scenery, and fast food. My father wanted to live on his own all the way to the end, but at what cost? My friends publicly marveled at what a good son I was but privately thought I was nuts.

It was my three-year-old who kept me sane. Michael rose to the occasion, getting in the car to make the tortuous weekend ride—Julie and I had jobs and had to be back on Monday—to and from Palm Springs with little if any complaint. He was, in fact, the only person who could consistently put Ellie in a good mood. I often found myself apologizing to my little boy for putting him through all this difficulty, but he, mature beyond his years, consoled me by saying, "Don't worry, Daddy. Everything's going to be okay." And he always wanted to come along with us; he was still at the stage where anytime we went somewhere without him, he was sure that we were out partying.

Michael and I during this period

Ellie had recently been diagnosed with the wet form of macular degeneration. His doctor explained that the condition caused the blood leakage in his eyes that was clouding his vision. Unfortunately, my father saw it as mysterious writing on the walls, and repeatedly asked me to call Stan, his apartment manager, to *demand* that he stop letting in whoever was nefariously writing on the walls. He was convinced that I couldn't see it because it was written with special disappearing ink. I now recognized that I was fighting a losing battle, so I told him that I'd call Stan and take care of it. But, I never did.

My father has always been one of the most impatient people on earth. When I arranged for some of his neighbors—who mainly refused to take any money—to help him, he expected them to act like servants and drop everything in order to run his errands. If they didn't do what he wanted, when he wanted, he refused to have anything more to do with them.

At this point, his hearing aids, constantly pushed to the limit, were malfunctioning at the worst possible times, usually on a Friday afternoon before a three-day holiday. Where was the nearby audiologist on Friday? "Oh, he plays golf and leaves on Fridays at 2:00 p.m. on the *dot*," said his secretary. God had better help those who get sick on a Friday afternoon, because you can bet that no one else but Him is going to be available.

Inquiries to Medicare about new hearing aids were fruitless. The powerful hearing aids that Ellie needed were too expensive and weren't covered. Audiology is a second-class citizen in the world of elder care, and believe it or not, until recently, Microsoft Word had the correct spelling of audiology as a spelling *mistake.*

As is common, the more my father's dementia took over, the more insistent he became that he was fine. Ellie's answers to our concerns or offers of help were something along the lines of "Mind your own damn business." The weekend round-trip car rides from the Bay Area to Palm Springs were crushing. We'd arrive around 10:00 p.m. like an all-night janitorial service and usually wouldn't finish until about two in the morning; while Michael fell asleep in front of cartoons carried from home, Julie and I cleaned every surface of the apartment.

The evidence of his deterioration was nauseating, and during one visit while we were having breakfast after an all-night drive, Ellie suddenly and without warning got up and ran (if you could call it that) to the bathroom.

Julie said, "You've got to go with him."

On my way to the bathroom, I started asking myself whether the cleaning of his house, and now his body, to allow him to live on his own was anything more than just a fool's errand.

Since my mother died, there hadn't been a piece of fruit or a fresh vegetable within a hundred yards of my father's house. No matter what I said, his version of "health food" was smoked salmon followed by a Planter's salted cashews chaser, and the lack of a balanced diet only served to sour his moods, worsen his skin, and hasten other already deteriorating conditions.

On each visit we'd shop for food, but trips to the supermarket with Ellie often turned into public arguments about diet and health. Always loudly and sometimes in front of strangers, he insisted that we should just *leave him alone.* Hot dogs, ham, raisin bread, smoked fish, and sliced turkey were his staples. When I went shopping without him, he became insulted and angry because he felt like I was saying that he couldn't take care of himself anymore; not to mention the fact that he absolutely hated the food choices that I knew were best for him.

It was a miracle that he learned how to use the microwave to cook his hot dogs, because he had virtually no kitchen (or mechanical) skills at all. This was someone who, when two-line phones were first introduced in the early 1960s, didn't understand that he had to push the "hold" button *before* you could go and answer the other line. No matter how many times we told him, when another call came in, he disconnected whomever he was first talking to. You could hear them screaming into the phone when my father said he had another call coming in, "No! Ellie, don't hang up the pho—!" But it was too late.

My father's mobility was becoming a real question mark, and I suggested that a cane might be a big help to him. He was emphatic. "Forget it!" I argued with him, saying that it made sense *in spite* of what he said.

For Ellie, those were fightin' words.

He became so furious with me that he started hopping up and down like an Olympic athlete and yelled, "I'd rather fall and kill myself before I'd use a goddamn cane!" It was almost (but not quite) comical—he'd actually rather be dead than risk being perceived as a hobbled old man.

In his fantasy of himself, he wanted to live fast, die young, and have a good-looking corpse. He had married a great-looking gal, had made and spent a lot of money, and didn't really care about anything else. The only problem was that he was still alive. He reminded me of the old Woody Allen joke, "If I'd known I was going to live this long, I'd have taken better care of my teeth."

Sometimes it's the service people you regularly meet with that end up knowing you best. They're often the ones who see the daily upswings and downturns and listen to the tales of small triumphs and occasional disappointments. This was certainly true of my parents, who were many years removed from their original sets of friends. I heard more compassion for them in the voices of their optometrist, their waiters, even their dry cleaner, than from the local friends of theirs with whom I would occasionally come into contact. My parents had just been too proud to confide in their current friends and, ultimately, felt more comfortable talking openly with the waitresses, grocers, and handymen that they encountered. They one and all delighted in my mother's beauty, grace, and charm, while being amused by my father's outsized personality and practiced storytelling.

Sometimes, my father had a hand in creating the story. Here's an example.

I was about seven years old when some distant cousins, who lived in Brooklyn, came out to our house on Long Island for a visit. They were sweet people, much less well-to-do than we were, and greatly appreciated a day in the country. The father of this family (a simple, quiet guy) was a WWII veteran who had fought extensively in Casablanca and all around North Africa. I personally witnessed the following conversation, later to be retold by my father many, many times:

ELLIE. Sammy, when you were in Casablanca, you must have gone to Rick's Café Américain.

SAMMY. No, Ellie. I went to every single joint there, but I never went to Rick's.

ELLIE. You never went to Rick's? How could that be? It's world famous—*everybody goes to Rick's*!

SAMMY, *perplexed.* Geez, Ellie. What can I tell you? I didn't go to Rick's.

ELLIE. How could anybody be dumb enough to be in Casablanca and not go to Rick's? It is impossible—you *must* have been there!

SAMMY. I don't think so. Too bad I missed it.

Sammy shrugged his shoulders and the conversation turned to other things.

A few nights later, my father called Sammy to ask him if he was still *absolutely* sure that he didn't stop at Rick's Café. Sammy, who probably felt like he missed the greatest nightclub in the world, told my father that if he ever went back, he wouldn't miss the chance to go to Rick's.

Once again, a few weeks later, my father called to ask Sammy if he'd finally figured out that he *must* have been to Rick's. By now, Sammy was frantic—how could he have missed this place?

Now, in those days, rerunning old movies on TV was just starting to pick up steam, and one night, the local channel ran that great classic *Casablanca*, starring Humphrey Bogart as the owner of *Rick's Café Américain*! The phone rang during the movie, and my father answered. It was Sammy.

ELLIE. Hello?

SAMMY. Ellie, you're a no good, dirty son of a bitch!

Ellie burst out laughing. My father had strung Sammy along, knowing that, eventually, he'd see *Casablanca* and figure it all out. Comedy that involved human suffering was Ellie's specialty, and my father got a *lot* of mileage out of that one.

Ellie most closely resembled a blend of famous TV characters Archie Bunker and Ralph Kramden, and like Ralph and Archie, he had a bit of a mean streak in his otherwise well-developed sense of humor. One Saturday, when I was about twelve or so, I asked my father if I could have some money to go bowling with my friends. He said, "How much do you need?" I said that I needed about ten dollars and he replied, "You need a ten? Here's a ten."

My brother approached next and asked him for some money to take his girlfriend out that night. My father asked, "How much do you need?" and my brother said he needed a twenty. My father replied, "You need a twenty? Here's a twenty."

My mother, standing nearby, asked for some cash to get a new dress at the local dress shop. He asked her how much it cost, and she said it was about a hundred dollars. Now, at that time a hundred dollars wasn't inexpensive, but neither was it a fortune for a high roller like Ellie. My father said, "A hundred dollars? Gladys, do you really need that dress?" My mother was shocked. "The little one asks for a ten, and you give him a ten. The big one asks for twenty and you give him a twenty. You give to your children but not to me?" she asked incredulously. My father said, "Gladys, them—they're my flesh and blood. But you? You're only a *paper* relative." He was laughingly implying that he and my mother were bound only by their marriage license.

We laughed, but it wasn't funny.

Chapter Three

Eventually, Ellie sought the help of a doctor in the hopes that medication would ease his hallucinations. The doctor gave him samples of Zyprexa, a powerful antipsychotic medicine used to treat schizophrenia and other psychotic disorders, but they weren't the right dosage. As usual, too impatient to wait for the nurse to break the pills in half for him, Ellie slipped out of the doctor's office and hustled a ride home from a stranger in the parking lot. Alone in his apartment, his arthritic hands were unable to break the pill, so he figured, *Why not?* and just took the whole pill.

I was aware that he was going to the doctor that day, and was waiting for him to call and tell me what had happened. When many hours passed without hearing from him, I knew something was wrong. I called Stan, the apartment manager, and asked him to check on Ellie. When Stan entered my father's apartment, he found Ellie lying on the floor in a semicomatose state. By the time Stan called me back, my father was already in the hospital.

I tracked him down by phone to the ER. A nurse informed me, "It was close," but they had managed to bring him back.

Bring him back? Bring him back to what? He had no companionship, had lost the ability to drive a car, and had a throat that didn't want to swallow any of the things he liked to eat. On top of it, he was hallucinating and slowly going deaf and blind. I said to her, "He's over ninety and has a DNR (do not resuscitate) on his record. What are you talking about?" She said, "Oh, sorry 'bout that. We didn't have time to check his records. It's a legal issue, you know."

Perfect irony—the DNR was the *only* thing in his entire life that he'd planned in advance, and it ended up being of no use at all.

For one second, I questioned whether or not he took the whole pill in an attempt at suicide, but that just wasn't Ellie. My father had an ego as big as all outdoors and thought he could handle *anything*. Simple as that.

About eight hours later, Julie, Michael, and I arrived at the hospital. The nurses gave me the name of the doctor who was in charge of my father's case and motioned me toward the waiting room. A few minutes later an MD came in and introduced himself. As I shook his hand, I noticed that his name didn't match the name I'd been given.

I asked him what had happened to the other doctor, and he replied, "You wouldn't want him. Trust me."

I wouldn't want him? I thought, *Wow, that's a strange answer.* I repeated the question.

More than a little annoyed, the doctor said, "Listen, that guy is in the business of saving the lives of forty-year-olds, *not ninety-three-year-olds.* If you want *me* to keep going while your father's vital signs have any strength at all, I'll try some things that he might respond to. What do you want to do?"

I was numb. Though my father's life had become one struggle after another, was I supposed to be his executioner? My mind screamed, *He was supposed to die! Why did you keep him alive?* I was now officially in hell—damned either way. I never wished him to die, and the answer to the doctor's question would probably be a no-brainer for most people—"Keep my father alive!" But it wasn't a no-brainer for me. He was angry and difficult, and I wondered if he'd even be glad to still be alive. But in the end, choosing death over life was impossible for me.

I heard myself mumble, "See what you can do."

The doctor kept Ellie alive—in a way. The effects of the Zyprexa left him in a semiconscious state, and though the nurses could shove food in his mouth and drag him to the bathroom, he was unable to open his eyes, speak, or respond intelligibly. And when the medical team saved his life, they tore his false teeth out and proceeded to lose them. He wasn't conscious enough to go to the dentist, but he couldn't really chew his food. I wanted to be with him if he either woke up or passed away, but I couldn't wait much longer. I had to return home soon.

The doctors and nurses confidently told me that it was probably just a matter of days, maybe a week or two at the most, until he passed. So before we left, Julie, Michael, and I turned off the lights, stood around his bed, and held each other's hands in prayer.

We continually checked on him after our return home, but within a short time, an administrator from the hospital called and said that they needed the bed. His condition was unchanged, and they couldn't keep him anymore. Once again, someone was telling me, "There's nothing more we can do."

The administrator referred me to a social worker who faxed me a list of skilled facilities that my father's insurance *might* pay for. But there were no spaces available for him in the places that I could afford, and the places that did have space for him charged a ton of money. I had no idea what to do and asked the hospital for more time. The hospital administration said no, but the social services people mentioned that someone not affiliated with the hospital was there and might be able to help me.

The social worker handed the phone to a woman who spoke in heavily accented English and introduced herself as Frances. In soothing tones, she said that she had a licensed board and care home in Palm Springs, would charge only my father's small Social Security check, and could take him in immediately. It seemed like a miracle to me, but I couldn't think logically at all and didn't question anything. All I knew was that someone had finally stepped in to help me with this unending, long-distance nightmare.

Frances moved Ellie into her home. He was still barely conscious and unable to open his eyes. She installed him in a room with another elderly man who never opened his mouth other than to eat. They made quite a pair. Also residing in the home was a sentient man who was unable to ever leave his bed, as well as a middle-aged female resident who sat and stared at the wall all day.

Frances' home was a nondescript tract house with popcorn ceilings, bad carpeting, and overstuffed, fake chenille furniture that was so soft you needed a crane to get out of the sofa and chairs. She was a short, slightly overweight, not unattractive Philippine woman of about fifty, and caring for the residents of her home served as her only business. I got the picture quickly when I saw the diet—mainly peanut butter and jelly sandwiches and a thin liquid that she tried to pass off as soup—that she served to her residents. Though the nutrition might have met the state's minimum requirements (frankly, I don't know what those standards are), the quality and variety of what she served them made me want to throw up. But no matter how many times I declined her offers, she'd still ask, "Do you want some?"

It suddenly dawned on me how my father had landed here. Frances trolled the local hospitals to find potential residents for her home! Duh! I had been completely demented and burned out from the whole experience and couldn't think rationally. All I had wanted was help.

Frances didn't actually *do* much of the work herself. She mainly employed her relatives to do the dirty work of assisting the residents. Most of them were in their late teens or early twenties and didn't want to be there in the first place. She spent most of her time in her bedroom, endlessly watching TV. Frances was pretty cagey; she was charming as hell when she needed you but tough as nails when she didn't.

Unfortunately, my father, dependent on her for proper food and medication, was getting thinner and thinner. It didn't seem to matter much to her—she continued to dole the food out with a thimble to elderly people who didn't have the capacity to complain. I was torn—while I wanted to hold her accountable and report her to *somebody*, most places wouldn't take only my father's small Social Security. I felt lousy that I wasn't rich and scared that, if I complained and had to move him, I might be forced into something worse.

Since my father wouldn't be able to live alone anymore, he no longer needed his apartment. My parents had always told me that, when they died, I would get forty, maybe even fifty thousand dollars for their custom-made furniture and collectibles. But after consulting with experts, I learned that all their cherished "antiques" were merely reproductions made in New York City in the '40s. What actually happened when I sold all the stuff was that an antique dealer who lived in my father's apartment complex gave me about four thousand dollars for everything. And I only got *that* much because the dealer knew Ellie and felt sorry for me.

The only thing that worried me was selling his clothes. He was always an absolute clothes *fanatic*, with a huge wardrobe, and even into his nineties, I had seen him trying on his outfits and admiring himself in the mirror. I said to Julie, "If he ever wakes up and asks where his clothes are, I'm dead."

She looked at me like I was crazy. "How can you worry about his clothes?" she asked.

But Julie didn't know him like I did, though I admit that at the time his chances of recovery seemed pretty remote. He couldn't speak intelligibly, didn't recognize me when I visited him, and wasn't showing any signs of improvement.

When I returned from a trip to visit him about four months into this period, my wife insisted that we finally had to get rid of the clothes. "We've waited long enough. We don't have room for all this stuff."

I caved in and gave away almost everything, keeping just a few of his favorite things to leave at Frances', mainly for appearances sake. A great camel hair sports jacket with leather buttons, a red and black checked jacket, and a British racing green suit with narrow lapels that I'd always loved were just a few of the prizes that I kept for him.

A few months later, the phone rang at my house. "Jamie??!!"

I was stunned; it was my father! He had come back to his senses after more than six months. "Dad, how are you? How are you feeling? Do you remember me coming to visit you these last months?"

He said, "Months? Feeling? What are you talking about? I feel fine!"

He didn't remember a thing, and Frances told me later that he had just woken up as if from a long sleep. I expected him to ask about what had happened to him or maybe something about his grandson. But he only had one question: "Jamie, I want to know something—*where the hell are all my clothes*??!!"

I looked at Julie and mouthed the words, *I hate you.*

Chapter Four

Ellie was back to his old self in the blink of an eye. He cajoled the attendants into letting him use their cell phones and berated them when they didn't hop to it fast enough. Because his regular exercise was fighting with Frances, I installed a hearing-impaired phone in his room to ease some of the strain between them. But when he called, the only things he wanted to know were, "Where are my clothes?" or "When are you coming?"

I was deathly afraid of telling him that I had given his cherished clothes away; the hurricane of fury he would unleash would be unbearable. So I lied. I told him that I had them "somewhere" and that I would "locate those damn boxes one way or another." I made it sound like I owned a warehouse filled with thousands of boxes.

Then the conversation would turn to Frances. "That bitch," he'd exclaim. "She thinks she's fooling me! I know they're stealing from me!" When I laughed and said that he had nothing left to steal, he responded, "My clothes! *They're stealing the rest of my clothes!*"

Drugs were Frances' first line of defense against Ellie's high-strung and demanding ways. She frequently requested permission to sedate him with prescriptions that she had amassed from her other residents. On one or two occasions, I let her give Ellie some medication to test the waters. But it never worked. They generally had the opposite effect on him, making him climb the walls at night instead of sleeping or relaxing. To complicate matters, he also had a common elderly condition known as "sundowning" where, with or without drugs, he slept in the day and was often awake at night.

When Frances called me, it was usually to ask if she could hammer him with even more drugs to quiet him down. After the first few times I said no, and I'd ask her if she was a nurse and could legally administer drugs to people. Her reply was always the same: "I am a *licensed* caregiver. I do what I think is best."

I once said to her, "Frances, executioners are licensed too. But they still have to wait for a court order." After that, she stopped trying to medicate my father.

Ellie had already figured out that Frances served mediocre cafeteria food, gave indifferent attention, and did as little as possible. Often she wasn't there at all, leaving her ill-prepared twenty-year-old nieces, nephews, and cousins in charge of the home and its residents. My father, perpetually angry that she wasn't providing the kind of care he expected, became more and more difficult to deal with. His perspective was that, since he was paying for it, he wanted the attention that he thought he was supposed to be getting. He wasn't entirely wrong, but it was absolutely lost on him that a little tact might have gotten him a lot further.

Ellie needed new dentures to replace the ones that the hospital staff had lost, but it was always a huge deal for Frances to arrange a dental visit for Ellie. "You know, I'm always just so *busy*," she said. When I confronted her about this and other issues, she acted like she was the Queen of England. "Remember, I am relieving the resident's families of an enormous burden," she often said, and she made it perfectly clear that she didn't care what *anybody* thought.

I never believed that Frances was actually evil, but I always came away thinking that, for her, giving good care was always going to be secondary to making money. During one conversation, she made her position clear. "Either take him or leave him," she told me, "but don't tell me how to run my home."

Keeping Ellie in Frances' home didn't have a lot of upside— he was unhappy with her, and she was unhappy with him. Whenever she tried to raise her rates, I'd call her bluff. "That's fine. No problem. We're ready to move on," I would say.

She never did follow through on her threat to up the price of my father's care, but in reality I had no idea where else I could take him. Though he'd recovered to a certain extent, he was still going to need *a lot* of help. But staying with Frances wasn't going to be a long-term solution because, to make a bad joke, she could *care less*.

At the end of the day, my complaints didn't accomplish anything other than making her angry. She was often on edge anyway because the turnover rate of her "employees" was so high that she always had someone new to break in.

We were on opposite sides—I was angling for better care at the same time she was trying to make a profit.

Other than my stopping Frances from overmedicating my father, she won the war; nothing ever changed.

The only remaining question was whether Ellie would die before I could get him into a better situation. I realized that he might not die anytime soon, and I could no longer take the time, expense, and difficulty of traveling to see him. Gary was reluctant to contribute much of anything (other than a little money), because he was against us paying attention to my father in the first place.

The downside of Gary's intellect is a certain cold-blooded selfishness. In our discussions about Ellie, my brother was consistent—ignore him. He advised me repeatedly that dealing with Ellie would be ultra-difficult, and in retrospect, he was clearly right—dealing with my father's demanding and sometimes abusive personality *was* an unbelievably arduous and difficult thing. But I just didn't have the same "off" button that Gary did. He can switch feelings and emotions on and off at will, and I can't. When I asked him whether ignoring our father was really a realistic approach, he said, "*I* definitely would." And he wasn't kidding. I was on my own.

I researched facilities in the Bay Area that would take my father's Medi-Cal and Social Security checks in exchange for room, board, and skilled care. I looked at tons of places and lots of different situations, but too often they smelled of urine or were just rundown, depressed environments. I eventually found out about the Jewish Home of San Francisco, a high-quality facility that accepted a certain amount of Medi-Cal residents among its full-pay population. But no beds were available, so we were put on a waiting list.

The charade was over; anger and irritation surfaced in almost every interaction between my father and Frances. Everybody was right, and everybody was wrong—Ellie was a major pain in the ass, but Frances was forever trying to chisel every extra cent out of her business. My father became so unhappy that he turned into a walking crisis, forever yelling about Frances, partly out of his frustration with her and partly because he just couldn't hear how unbelievably *loud* he was.

Sometimes I fought fire with fire, which occasionally made him realize what he sounded like. "What do you want me to do," I'd yell in frustration, "tell her that she's a son of a bitch?"

When he heard the words out of my mouth instead of his, they didn't sound so good to him. But Ellie was crazy like a fox—out of control when he wanted to be but sane when he needed to be.

After looking at "affordable" board and care facilities in Northern California, I finally settled on a home in Vallejo, a distant suburb of San Francisco, that wasn't fancy but was clean and relatively safe. I was pretty sure that my Brooklyn-born, New York Jewish father was going to hate it, but assisted-care choices for elderly people without money are few and far between.

After the experience with Frances, the burden of making decisions for my father felt onerous—what was I committing him to this time? The old men who lived at the home in Vallejo seemed nice and still reasonably *compos mentis*, but would they be compatible with my father's cantankerous, yet still occasionally personable, personality? Would anyone? At every facility I visited, he was an alien compared to the other residents. Yiddish? Forget about it. Matzo? When I asked various facilities if they could buy matzo (Jewish flat bread) for him, hardly any of them had ever even heard of it.

The Jewish Home still had no available spaces, and I kept thinking that somebody there has just got to *die* already. Ellie bitched and moaned about leaving Palm Springs but knew that, if he stayed, I could only visit him once or twice a year. Julie and I talked it over and decided that it might be best if she flew to get him while I looked after Michael. I crossed my fingers.

Ellie generally listened to Julie, far more than he listened to me anyway. A Hollywood worshiper his entire life, my father respected the fact that Julie had worked her way up the Hollywood ladder to big jobs and good bucks. To my father, I was merely a well-paid producer and director of television commercials and videos, which didn't exactly conjure up visions of Hollywood glamour for him. Ellie was more Hollywood than most of the actors I ever met.

He loved movies and had the attitude, the clothes, and the storytelling ability that fit into the bigger-than-life image he had of himself as a *star*.

Chapter Five

The day before Julie was scheduled to leave for Palm Springs, the phone rang in the middle of the afternoon. As I picked it up, the sky opened and a heavenly choir began to sing; the head of admissions for the Jewish Home was calling to say that a Medi-Cal bed had just become available and that Ellie's Social Security check would be enough to give him all the room, board, medical and nursing care he needed. Julie burst into tears.

A few days later, Julie flew to Palm Springs, packed up Ellie's few belongings, and brought him to San Francisco. I picked them up at San Francisco International Airport, selfishly taking Michael out of school to come with me because his presence kept my father calmer. We moved Ellie into a private room at the Jewish Home, plugged in his old TV, and put away some cartons of brassieres that he just *had* to keep on hand.

My father was one of those guys who could fit a woman for a bra like a doctor examines a patient. When I was a very little boy, I'd watch him do a "hands on" check to see if the cup fit properly, and whether or not a wired bra might be needed. The women at the corset shop were completely unmoved, and only worried about how they'd look at their son's bar mitzvah or their daughter's wedding.

When we moved him into the Jewish Home I asked him whether or not he really needed to keep the bras anymore. "Someone will need one; you'll see!" he said. Then he asked for a phone.

Uh-oh! I thought. *Here we go again.*

Michael, my father, Gary, and me at the Jewish Home

At first, life at the Jewish Home was a honeymoon; everything was beautiful and everyone was an angel. But all honeymoons come to an end, and after three or four months, his volatile temperament and frustrations with "the service" resurfaced. With Frances, he'd had some legitimate complaints, but the Jewish Home—though the food was industrial and the assisting staff inconsistent—did a good job of taking care of a lot of people. Ellie just never understood that he wasn't the only resident there.

The Jewish Home of San Francisco is worthy of note as an example of what is good in elderly care. It's a nonprofit, licensed, skilled nursing center specializing in care, services, and programs for older adults. The home provided skilled nurses, relatively competent doctors, full board, and reasonable care in a decent, not overly institutional environment that was like a hospital with separate apartments. Like always, the nurse's aides and attendants were the ones who actually took care of the residents. They were the true interface of the institution and did everything that wasn't medical in nature—cleaning, dressing, and attending to the residents; bringing those who couldn't walk to meals; accompanying residents to doctor appointments, dental visits, and trips for outside medical testing; and on and on.

Some of the aides were health care professionals, and they treated the residents with sincere kindness and great care. But it was a crapshoot; many aides were nonprofessionals or part-time workers for whom health care had nothing to do with their future lives. Too few treated the residents as individuals with unique needs, and some seemed only vaguely aware that they were dealing with actual human beings. Many of the assistants who attended to Ellie seemed mainly concerned with executing their duties as quickly as possible. Nurses' aides are responsible for showering, bathing, and applying topical ointments, but shoving an old person in and out of the shower as fast as possible wasn't the answer. I often overheard the lady next door to Ellie saying to the attendants "Don't be so rough!" While a lot of the nonprofessionals came and went as fast as they could, the professional aides *never* rushed, knowing that gentle, sensitive attention was an essential component of caring for the elderly.

Communication was the biggest issue. Though serving a mainly English-speaking population, many aides didn't have a professional command of the language. They often consulted with each other in Russian, Tagalog (a language of the Philippines), or Spanish before responding to questions in badly broken English. It gave everything a conspiratorial ring, and I often couldn't help thinking, *Is there something they're not telling me?*

I brought the language issue up with the administrators and head nurses during our family care meetings. The response was always the same: the aides weren't supposed to speak a foreign language.

Unfortunately, this remained an unresolved issue.

The RNs (registered nurses), an international group hailing from China, Russia, the Philippines, Taiwan, Panama and the United States, were absolutely great. All had, at minimum, a professional command of English and were compassionate; attentive to detail; and very, very good at their jobs. Their knowledge, professionalism and caring greatly reassured the often anxious residents and their families.

The doctors were either mediocre or great, depending on your point of view. If you wanted your parent to have ample pain and sleep medication, then they were great. But it was a far different story if you were interested in a healthier, less drug-oriented approach. They first put Ellie on Seroquel, a drug mainly used to treat schizophrenia, and it made his dementia much, much worse. Then they tried Aricept, a medication often used for Alzheimer's and memory loss, and all it did was drug Ellie into a state of total incoherency. When I mentioned vitamin supplements and diet therapies, the doctors looked at me like I had just landed from Mars. Though drugs were having a detrimental and weakening effect on my father, the doctors weren't averse to suggesting a bit of morphine to keep him "comfortable." It seemed like prescribing what they called "comfort care"—the administration of drugs that dulled the pain along with the mind and the senses—was much, much easier for them.

All the choices were bad because Ellie still reacted poorly to a whole host of medications. He still had intermittent hallucinations, but antipsychotics, as well as antibiotics for his bladder infections, made him completely crazy or utterly incoherent. Sleeping pills frequently kept him awake. In the end, I got the medical staff to stop drugging my father, and while he didn't get a lot better, he also didn't get much worse. Most importantly, he was still *himself*—not the drugged-out, incoherent, "comfortable" version. I must say that some of the doctors reminded me a lot of beatnik Maynard G. Krebs from the old Dobie Gillis show—"What? Me?? Work???"

Talking about things like food and laundry may sound trivial compared to omnipresent life-and-death issues, but they're not. They sometimes represent the last bits of personal expression and sensory enjoyment that a very aged person might have. Unfortunately, the industrial-type laundry at the Jewish Home was dreadful, either delivering the wrong stuff or just simply losing more of my father's clothes altogether. Ellie kept track of his clothes like a bookie keeps track of the day's races, and now positively stricken at the thought of losing his remaining wardrobe, Ellie refused to change his clothes.

"My clothes are perfectly clean!" he'd scream, but his eyesight had gotten so bad that he couldn't see the food stains that were all over him.

Julie and I didn't have the time to do his daily laundry, but we often took his prized sweaters and shirts home for careful cleaning. That made him really happy. But since the laundry at the Jewish Home just massacred everything else, Ellie's clothes continued to be an ongoing issue (and nightmare) for me.

As for the food, although they did have *plenty* of matzo, the Jewish Home obviously figured that old people's taste buds died before they did. The food was generally boiled into submission before being put through a de-flavorizer, and we tried to supplement his diet by bringing him everything from Ensure to cookies and breads that Julie baked at home. When the Jewish Home brought a meal into Ellie's room, he'd try it and say, "Taste this food! It's lousy!"

Sometimes, to make him happy, I'd have to taste the meal—chalky mashed potatoes, overdone vegetables, and some sort of meat covered in a brown sauce that you could repair highways with.

After I left, I'd have to go out and buy myself a new tongue.

My father's dementia never became a fully 24-7 condition, and before I realized that it came and went, I thought that maybe he's just *pretending* to be delusional. But his daily stories about how the walls moved each night to reveal grand nightclubs hosting boisterous parties on the other side told me otherwise. He described his conversations at the clubs in great detail, telling me how he and the other guests hashed over their business deals, their wives, and where they were going on upcoming vacations. One day I asked him how he could have gotten to all these nightclubs and parties, since he hadn't left his bed for days on end. He said, "I don't remember … Who cares? But don't worry. I was there!"

One day Ellie asked me for fifty bucks in cash. I was surprised because there was no need for money at the Jewish Home, whose policy strongly discouraged residents from having cash. He told me that it was so he could pay Archie back for the cab he had to take home from the bar last night.

"Archie? Who's Archie?" I asked.

He said, "You know, Archie! Archie Bunker! He's become a very good friend. He's sommmmmmmme character! But sometimes he annoys me."

Assurances to my father that there were no magic walls, that he was simply asleep and dreaming of a beloved TV character, only antagonized him. Ever more frequent bladder infections made him increasingly agitated and confused. At first, I thought it was better to fight the onset of his condition rather than "give in" to it. But I was wrong—it was already way too late for fighting.

Ellie was now over ninety-five, alternately cantankerous or delusional with an occasional side dish of lucidity. His hearing aids, taxed to the max, were more than ever in need of costly and time-consuming repairs. The staff audiologist only came in once a week and was always behind. She was so backed up that it was next to impossible to get in to see her, and once, I sarcastically asked her whether Ellie was the first hearing-impaired person who'd ever lived at the Jewish Home. She just gave me a resigned shrug.

When my father, no matter how slightly, could hear me, I could tell that it made him feel like he was still present, still *here*, still part of the world.

But now it was the worst of all worlds; I was forced to communicate with him by writing in black marker on a white

Michael, around the time my father passed away

erasable board, while holding it closely in front of his now more-gray-than-blue eyes.

I brought Michael to visit my father as often as possible, and some-times he helped bring Ellie back to reality, kind of "shocking" him into present time and place. Despite his encroaching dementia, he never forgot that he was Ellie Legon or that Michael was his grandson. When my father was lucid, he talked to Michael and I about the times when he was a little boy growing up in Brooklyn, when present-day stores and busy streets were farms and today's strip malls were fine Victorian brownstones. When I mentioned my mother, he would have little, if anything, to say; it seemed like that chapter was over, done with, and in no need of further discussion. His mind was increasingly back among the people that he loved the most—his mother, father, and siblings. He left today's world behind to travel into the happier memories of other days where, as the youngest of five, he idolized his siblings and mythologized his parents.

He sat and told us once again about the times his father brought strolling musicians into the house to play for the family during dinner, or when his brother, Solly, who could kick the crap out of anybody, ruled the neighborhood. Sometimes he talked about all the fun he had with the animals that lived in his giant yard, or he'd lovingly recall his mother, an oasis of gentility amidst a gang of crazy Russian hustlers. She was the only person in his family who was sensitive to my father, but she died of cancer when he was only seventeen. I don't think he ever got over it.

Though Ellie could hardly get out of bed, he still asked for the money to pay for the cab rides he took to and from Archie's Place. It was also becoming harder and harder for him to remember who I was; sometimes I was still his son, but at other times, he thought I was one of his brothers. I got used to playing whatever part was necessary to make the situation as comfortable as possible.

A baseball fan his entire life, the thing he loved to do most was watch his little grandson swing a baseball bat by the foot of his bed. "Oh, he's got a good swing!" he'd say.

Chapter Six

As his ninety-seventh birthday approached, Ellie was unable to get to the bathroom without assistance. But one day, as stubborn as ever, he tried to go by himself and fell on the linoleum floor. He'd fallen many times before but had always escaped injury. This time, he wasn't so lucky, and he broke his hip. Already being so frail, he came down with pneumonia within a few days.

Ellie had beaten death so many times before that it was hard to think of him as actually *dying*. He was such a volcanic energy that, even in old age, he still retained the core of the person who my friends in high school had called Ellie the Lion.

Then, two weeks after the pneumonia set in, the social worker from the Jewish Home called and said that we'd better come over right away.

We rushed over and found my father with his eyes closed, breathing very slowly and with great difficulty. For what would be the last time, Michael, Julie, and I stood around his bed and prayed. I said to Michael (eight years old at the time) that he had the option to wait outside, but he stopped me and said, "I've been with you and Papa [the name he called my father] all the time. I'm not going to leave now."

I removed Ellie's watch from his wrist—he was a watch lover who hated being without one—and whispered, "Time is over now, Pop."

We settled down and waited. The social worker stopped by and told us that she was sure that he could hear us and that we should continue to talk to him. So we talked. We told him that we loved him, that he shouldn't worry about us, and that he should allow himself to go. His breathing grew shallower and shallower, and we had the sense that the moment was upon us.

At that *exact* second, a high-pitched Hitchcockian scream came from the delusional lady resident in the next room—"Eeeeeyahhhhhhh!" It was timed so perfectly and was so surreal that we all looked at each other and burst out laughing—a perfect comedic moment for Ellie, a lifelong comedy fan. And then, a few seconds later and only two weeks after contracting pneumonia, Ellie the Lion was gone.

I stood up and stared at him. Julie moved toward the telephone, saying that she was going to call the nurse. I looked at her and said, "Don't touch that phone, because if anybody is gonna come back from the dead, it's gonna be him."

We sat and waited a few more minutes, but this time, he really was gone. I was overwhelmed with a mix of both grief and relief. My father had always said, "It'll be easier for you when I'm gone," and while Ellie was more than difficult to handle, he was still the only father I'll ever have.

A nurse came into the room and pronounced my father dead. More nurses quickly arrived and made a tourniquet that helped Ellie's jaw stay closed, preventing his face from freezing into a contorted death mask. I stared into space while they took his body away, feeling completely blank and empty. We gathered up his possessions, donating as much as we could to the home and keeping the remaining pictures and mementos that had meaning for us. We said our good-byes to the earthly remains of my father, and when we made our farewells to the nurses and caregivers, I could tell that, even they, practiced in dealing with death, felt some small measure of loss. They told us that they'd miss us, and then we walked out of the Jewish Home for the last time and into the surreal light of mourning to begin the grieving process.

Conclusion

My father was right—his passing was a relief, not only for my family but I think for him as well. His struggle was finally over, and we were left only with a funny sense of withdrawal in our now much quieter household.

Looking back, I realize that the most important aspect of what we did for my father was that we paid close attention to him. It's far too easy for old people to get caught in the net of a highly impersonal system. They're often too frail, too weak, or too infirm to be able to advocate for themselves. Many are without proper advocates—a relative, a friend, or even just a kindly neighbor who can speak on their behalf. Ellie was lucky; he had Julie, Michael, and me. In today's broken health care system, being taken care of often has too little to do with *being paid attention to.*

It was Julie's unswerving dedication to her family that helped steady a very rocky ship that was sailing on a difficult voyage into the unknown. In spite of her being from a completely

Julie

different, Middle American background, she loved my mother and could appreciate my father's big personality. She was no pushover daughter-in-law. She fought Ellie when he was unreasonable, but she still went to visit him when I just couldn't face him. She called the nurses to check on him when we couldn't be there and looked in on him at the Jewish Home during some of her lunch hours to keep him calm. In some ways, she became his main advocate, but Ellie instinctively knew that he couldn't abuse her—she was only going to take so much from him and no more.

***

Here's my two-cent rant: Assisted or skilled caregiving is part work and part calling. Caring for those who can no longer care for themselves is a sensitive situation, and I didn't want some twenty-year-old, tattooed hipster who didn't give a damn taking care of my father. Too many people in these jobs are underpaid, undertrained, and only passing through on their way to somewhere else. The rigorous oversight needed to control the private caregivers who cut too many corners is virtually nonexistent. Care for the aged needs to be a nonprofit, privately run program that is part of a revamped, not-for-profit, health care system. The whole health care industry needs to be run in the same way successful nonprofit foundations are run—controlled costs, clear rules, and strict regulations governing conduct and operations. High-level assisted or skilled care should be available to everyone, not just the wealthy.

***

Ellie was disappointed that I didn't have enough money to set him up in style, and I know that he felt forced to give in to assisted-care living. He never understood the reality that receiving good care wasn't something that he was automatically entitled to. In the end, he actually had a relatively positive outcome from what could be, and is for many people, an awful experience. In America, good care is something that you either purchase or else do without.

The debate about health care is all about survival and liability. The current system keeps people alive mainly to prevent lawsuits and salve our collective guilty conscience. In the (small) amount of public debate about quality of life issues, the prevailing theory among the health care industry, and the general population, seems to be that it's better to be alive at all costs rather than dead. But I'm not so sure. And because too many families are unable or unwilling to supervise the care of their parents, the elderly person can easily end up at the mercy of for-profit providers willing to cut corners to meet their bottom line.

Caring for my father during his decline was a difficult experience. I was forced to discover truths about my parents, the aging process, and myself that were sometimes surprising and frequently uncomfortable. My son learned valuable lessons about people young and old but was also exposed to a lot more anxiety and frustration than I would have liked. Looking back, it seems that managing these situations requires a skill set that's a cross between those of a nurse, a butler, and a Buddhist monk.

And because everyone's situation is different, giving advice to people who are taking care of aging parents is tricky; no one-size-fits-all solutions exist for these situations. But I will say this much: without a supportive partner, wife, husband, sibling, or friend, caring for an elderly parent is an *exponentially* more difficult experience. You need someone to talk things out with who can help you make sense of the situation. Making decisions for another human being, let alone your parents, is one of the most difficult things you can do, and I personally think that the people who have to go it alone have an even harder time. If one doesn't already exist, someone should create a support network for the single children of aging parents.

I still remember the deal that I made with my dad when I was a little boy. I was about eight, and we were in the car together on the way to visit one of his customers, a corset shop in Brooklyn. I said, "Dad, when I'm sixty years old, you'll be a hundred. If you have to go when I'm sixty, then you can go—*but not before then*!" He laughed and promised he would do the best he could. I would say he did a pretty good job of keeping that promise.

Ellie didn't have a sensitive bone in his body, and though I had much love for him as a father, I can't say that I ever really liked him as a person. But that had nothing to do with the reasons why I, to the best of my ability, took care of him. I did it not only because he was my father and had taken good care of me at the beginning of my life (a good reason in and of itself), but also because I wanted to set a positive example for my son about the importance of giving to, and taking care of, other people. And it was, without a doubt, the right thing to do. I know that Michael would do the same for me and that he'll pass these lessons on to his children. And last but not least, I didn't want my son to be uncomfortable with old people because, God knows, I'm *already* old ...

I'll be ninety on July 1. I can't wait to
be ninety! Another victory!
—Olivia de Havilland, Oscar-winning actress,
speaking in 2006

About the Author

Jamie Legon began his career in the entertainment business producing concerts in South America. He then moved to Hollywood, where he produced and directed commercials and videos of all kinds during a twenty-five year span. Mr. Legon lives in Northern California with his family.